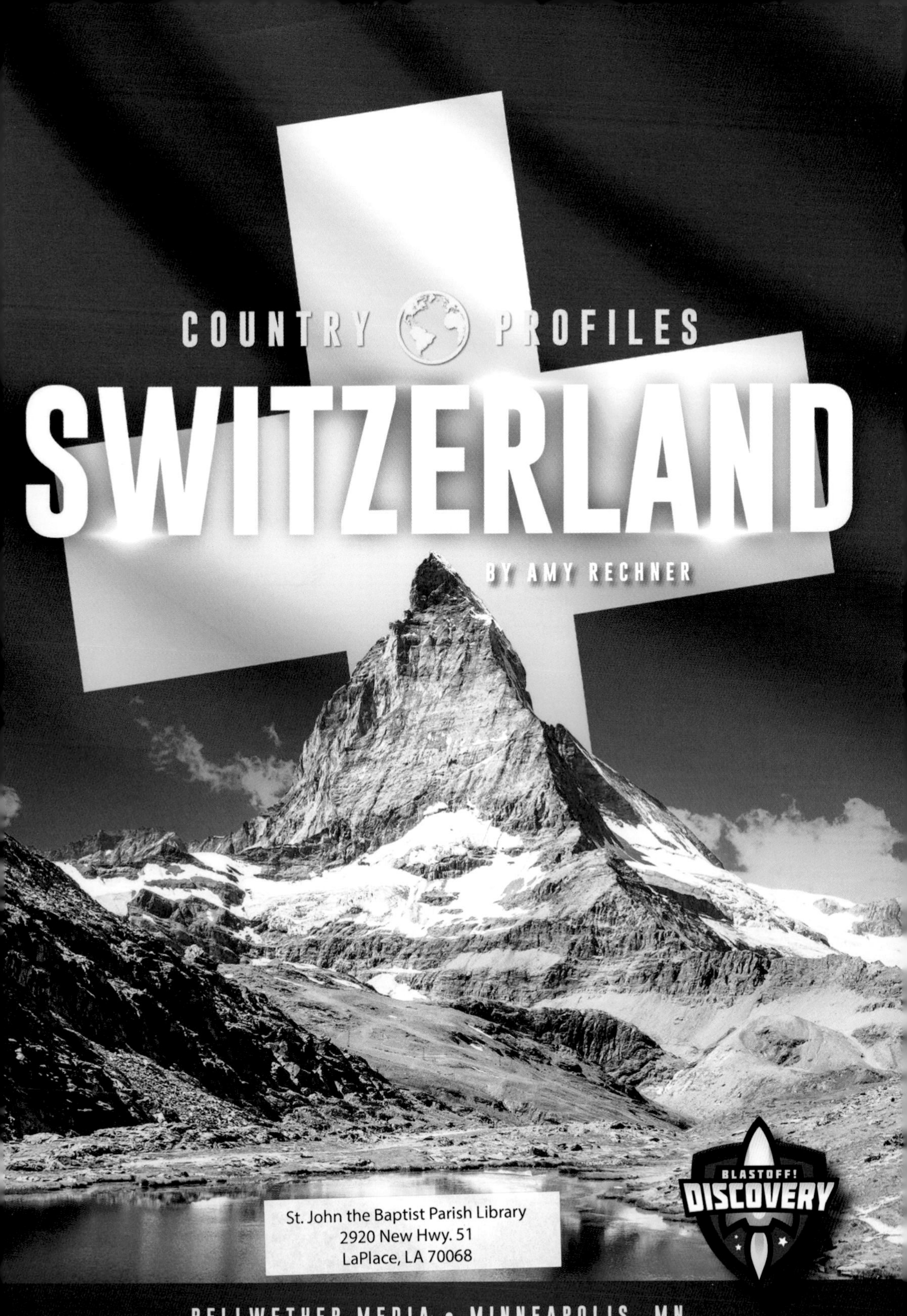

COUNTRY 🌎 PROFILES

SWITZERLAND

BY AMY RECHNER

BLASTOFF!
DISCOVERY

BELLWETHER MEDIA • MINNEAPOLIS, MN

Blastoff! Discovery launches
a new mission: reading to learn.
Filled with facts and features, each
book offers you an exciting new
world to explore!

This edition first published in 2019 by Bellwether Media, Inc.

No part of this publication may be reproduced in whole or in part
without written permission of the publisher.
For information regarding permission, write to Bellwether Media, Inc.,
Attention: Permissions Department,
6012 Blue Circle Drive, Minnetonka, MN 55343.

Library of Congress Cataloging-in-Publication Data

Names: Rechner, Amy, author.
Title: Switzerland / Amy Rechner.
Description: Minneapolis, MN : Bellwether Media, Inc., 2019. |
   Series: Blastoff! Discovery: Country Profiles | Includes
   bibliographical references and index.
Identifiers: LCCN 2018039195 (print) | LCCN 2018040104 (ebook)
   | ISBN 9781681036823 (ebook) | ISBN 9781626179646
   (hardcover : alk. paper)
Subjects: LCSH: Switzerland–Juvenile literature.
Classification: LCC DQ17 (ebook) | LCC DQ17 .R33 2019 (print) |
   DDC 949.4–dc23
LC record available at https://lccn.loc.gov/2018039195

Editor: Rebecca Sabelko   Designer: Brittany McIntosh

Printed in the United States of America, North Mankato, MN.

TABLE OF CONTENTS

One sunny, summer morning, a family boards a train in the city of Grindelwald. Carrying winter jackets and mittens, they enjoy the Alpine scenery as the train climbs Jungfrau Mountain. It goes through a long tunnel and stops for a view of a **glacier** called the Sea of Ice. Before long, they are at the *Jungfraujoch*, the Top of Europe.

JUNGFRAUJOCH

OTHER TOP SITES

ALBERT EINSTEIN HOUSE

LION OF LUCERNE

PIZ GLORIA RESTAURANT

ST. PIERRE CATHEDRAL

They explore the elaborate Ice Palace. White snow crunches underfoot as they climb to the Sphinx Observatory. They admire the views as cold air reddens their cheeks. Snowcapped mountaintops tower overhead while summery flowers bloom below. This is Switzerland!

Switzerland is a small country in the heart of Europe. It separates the northern and southern regions of the continent. Switzerland covers only 15,937 square miles (41,277 square kilometers). The capital, Bern, is in the west-central part of the **landlocked** country.

Germany lines Switzerland's northern border. Austria is to the east. The tiny country of Liechtenstein is sandwiched between Austria and Switzerland on the eastern border. Italy lies to the south. France wraps around Switzerland's curvy western border.

FRANCE

THE RHINE TRIANGLE

The borders of Germany, France, and Switzerland all meet at a point. It is in the middle of the Rhine River in the city of Basel, about 60 miles (97 kilometers) north of Bern.

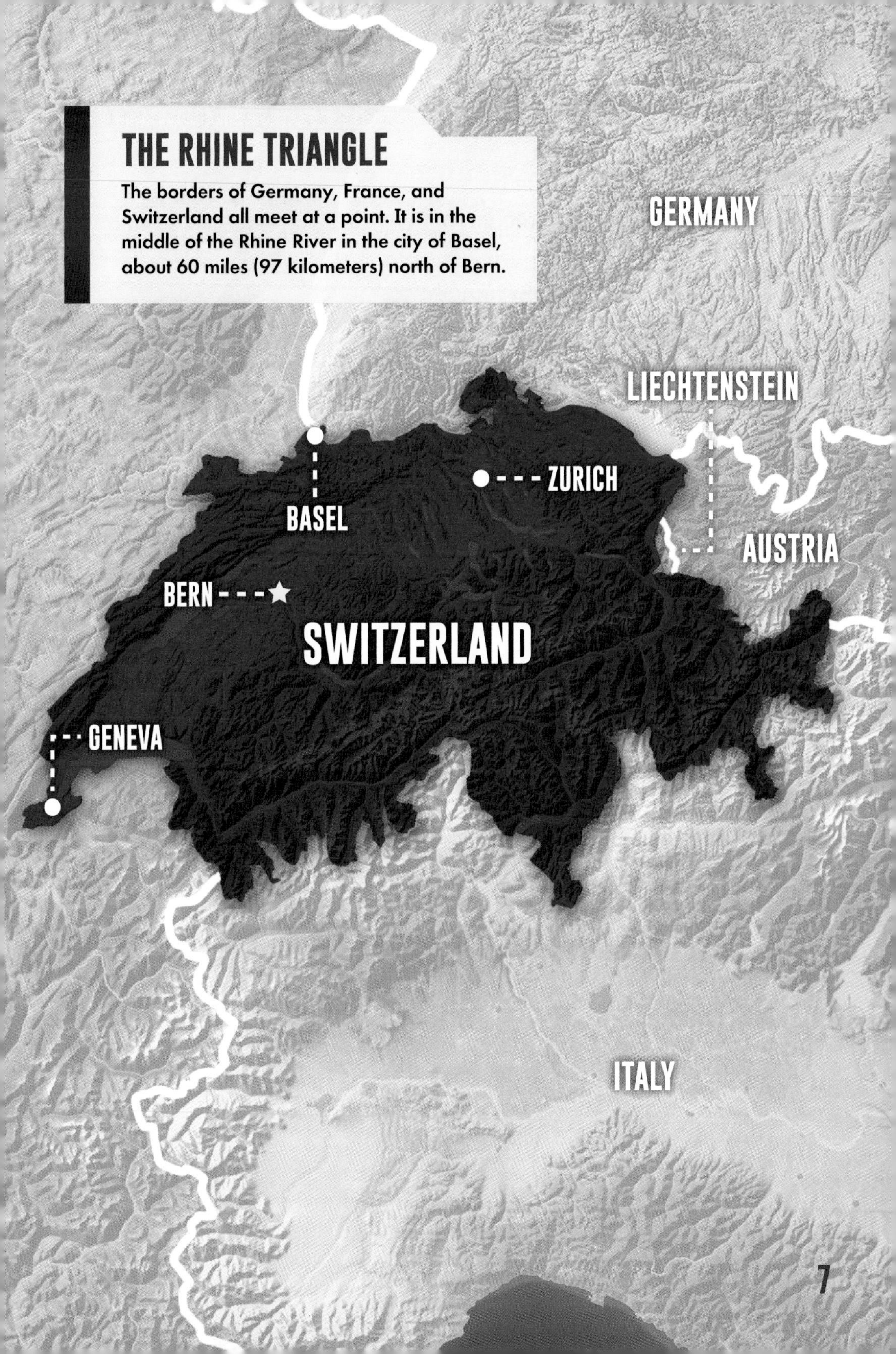

GERMANY

LIECHTENSTEIN

ZURICH

BASEL

AUSTRIA

BERN - - - ★

SWITZERLAND

GENEVA

ITALY

LANDSCAPE AND CLIMATE

= THE ALPS = JURA MOUNTAINS

RHINE RIVER

N
W — E
S

The Alps cover more than half of Switzerland. These mountains stretch from the southwest to the east and into neighboring countries. The Jura Mountains run along the northwestern French border. Switzerland's longest river, the Rhine, follows the northern border. Central Switzerland is a **plateau** called the Mittelland. Rivers run across its green hills and valleys.

MITTELLAND
BERN

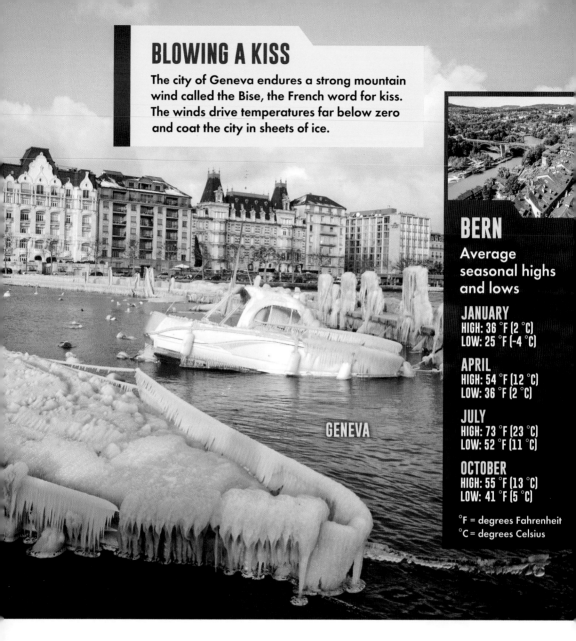

BLOWING A KISS

The city of Geneva endures a strong mountain wind called the Bise, the French word for kiss. The winds drive temperatures far below zero and coat the city in sheets of ice.

GENEVA

BERN

Average seasonal highs and lows

JANUARY
HIGH: 36 °F (2 °C)
LOW: 25 °F (-4 °C)

APRIL
HIGH: 54 °F (12 °C)
LOW: 36 °F (2 °C)

JULY
HIGH: 73 °F (23 °C)
LOW: 52 °F (11 °C)

OCTOBER
HIGH: 55 °F (13 °C)
LOW: 41 °F (5 °C)

°F = degrees Fahrenheit
°C = degrees Celsius

The climate varies greatly depending on **elevation**. Icy glaciers scrape across mountaintops. The plateau has a **temperate** climate with a lot of winter fog. Palm trees grow in the warm temperatures along the Italian border.

The mountains of Switzerland shelter many kinds of animals. Alpine ibex with long, curved horns munch on leaves and grass. Chamois have sharp hooves to climb steep mountain faces.

Red deer roam the forests. Wolves and lynx are more rare. Marmots **burrow** their way to safety as golden eagles and red foxes hunt for prey. Bearded vultures circle in the sky, waiting for leftovers. Songbirds like nuthatches and larks sing through the warmer seasons in trees and bushes. Loons and grebes mingle with ducks and geese on the lakes.

ALPINE IBEX

RED DEER

ALPINE MARMOT

WOOD NUTHATCH

GREAT CRESTED GREBES

BEARDED VULTURE

BEARDED VULTURE

Life Span: 21 years
Red List Status: near threatened

bearded vulture range =

LEAST CONCERN	NEAR THREATENED	VULNERABLE	ENDANGERED	CRITICALLY ENDANGERED	EXTINCT IN THE WILD	EXTINCT

TRADITIONAL
SWISS CLOTHES

Around 8 million people call Switzerland home. Most live in the country's central region. The population covers a huge range of **ethnicities**. One in five residents of Switzerland is from a different country. Some are **refugees** seeking safety. Half of the foreign residents are from Italy, Germany, Portugal, and France.

Switzerland has four official languages. German is the most widely used, followed by French, Italian, and Romansch. Many people speak more than one language. Many Swiss are Catholics or Protestants. Small numbers follow Islam or Judaism. About one in four Swiss do not practice any religion.

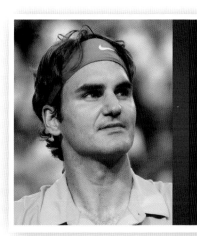

FAMOUS FACE

Name: Roger Federer
Birthday: August 8, 1981
Hometown: Basel, Switzerland
Famous for: Known as the world's best tennis player, he has won 20 Grand Slams and funds education programs in Africa and Switzerland through the Roger Federer Foundation

SPEAK GERMAN

ENGLISH	GERMAN	HOW TO SAY IT
hello	hallo	HA-lo
goodbye	auf wiedersehen	owf VEE-der-zane
please	bitte	BIT-eh
thank you	danke	DAHNK-eh
yes	ja	YAH
no	nein	NINE

ZURICH

ZURICH

Family plays an important role in Swiss life. The typical Swiss family has one or two children. Grandparents often live nearby or with the family and help with childcare. Three-quarters of Switzerland's residents live in **urban** areas. Most city dwellers live in apartments. Many use buses, trains, and trams to get around.

Houses are more common in **rural** areas. Many are modern. But some are more **traditional**, like the Swiss mountain *chalet*. Trains zoom across the country, sometimes going through tunnels in the Alps. The Gotthard Base Tunnel is more than 35 miles (57 kilometers) long!

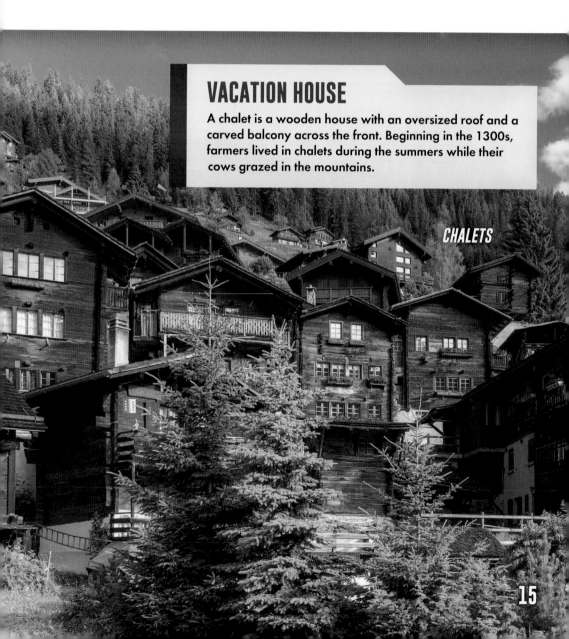

VACATION HOUSE

A chalet is a wooden house with an oversized roof and a carved balcony across the front. Beginning in the 1300s, farmers lived in chalets during the summers while their cows grazed in the mountains.

CHALETS

The Swiss are polite and friendly. Cheek kisses are shared with close friends and family. Being on time and holding doors for people are important to the Swiss. Activities like gum chewing and hair brushing in public are considered impolite.

TALK, TALK, TALK

Although German is the most common official language, many Swiss also speak a regional version called Swiss-German. It is hard for German speakers to understand!

ALPENHORNS

Switzerland has a rich **heritage** in folk music. Most towns have **amateur** bands that play traditional dance music. Choral groups sing and **yodel**. The **alpenhorn**, once used by shepherds to call to one another from mountains, is played at festivals.

17

Swiss children start school at age 4. That is followed by six years of primary school. After three years of lower secondary school, students decide their future path. They choose between an upper school that prepares them for a job, or a *gymnasium*, which prepares them for university.

More than three-quarters of Swiss workers have **service jobs**. Banking is one of the country's largest industries. Many people serve **tourists** at ski **resorts** or other attractions. Swiss factories make watches, machinery, and chemicals. There are few farmers in Switzerland.

MOUNTAIN GUIDE

WATCH MAKER

CLOCK WATCHERS
Thirty million watches are made in Switzerland each year!

ICE HOCKEY

The Swiss are great fans and players of ice hockey and soccer, which they call football. Both downhill and cross-country skiing are very popular, too. The Alps attract mountain climbers, bikers, and hikers. Switzerland's many lakes fill up with summer swimmers and winter ice skaters.

DOWNHILL SKIING

20

When they are not spending time outdoors, the Swiss enjoy movies, music, and spending time with family. Cooking is a popular hobby. Having friends over to share a meal is a welcome weekend event.

COOKING

TSCHAU SEPP

Number of players: 2-5

What You Need:

- one deck of playing cards, with the numbers 2, 3, 4, and 5 removed in all suits.

Instructions:

1. Each player gets six cards. All the remaining cards are stacked in the center. The top card is turned over and put next to the stack.

2. The player on the dealer's left goes first. They need to top the upturned card with one that is the same suit or the same number. If they don't have one, they draw from the deck. If the card they draw doesn't work, they keep it. Then it is the next player's turn.
   - If an 8 is put at the top of the pile, the next person skips their turn.
   - If a 10 is put down, the direction of play goes in reverse, to the right.
   - If an ace is put down, the player gets another turn.
   - Jacks are wild! They can always be used. The player can also decide the suit of the next card to be placed.

3. If the stack of cards is used up, the turned-up cards are shuffled and put down as a new stack.

4. When a player puts their second-to-last card down, they announce, "Tschau!" (pronounced CHOW). If this step is missed, the player must take another card. The player who gets rid of all of their cards first wins. When the last card is laid down, the winner says, "Sepp!"

CHEESE *FONDUE*

IT'S THE CHEESIEST

Switzerland produces many kinds of cheese. The Swiss cheese with holes is called *Emmentaler*, a German name. Other cheeses have French or Italian names that reflect the area where they are made.

A light breakfast of bread with butter and jam often starts the day. A favorite cooked breakfast is a potato pancake called *rösti*. Lunch is often a sandwich. Dinner is meat or fish served with salad and potatoes or pasta. A favorite pasta is *spaetzli*, which are gumdrop-sized bites covered in butter.

Cheese *fondue* is a traditional Swiss dish. Chunks of bread on long forks are dipped into a pot of rich, melted cheese. Desserts can be fancy **tortes** or a simple, perfect piece of Switzerland's famous chocolate.

RÖSTI

SPAETZLI

BIRCHER MÜESLI

Ingredients:
2 cups rolled or quick oats
1 3/4 cups milk
1/4 cup apple juice
3 tablespoons lemon juice
1 apple
1-2 tablespoons honey
1 1/2 cups plain yogurt
A dash of cinnamon (optional)
Your choice of toppings: berries, sliced bananas, dried fruits, nuts, raisins, coconut, etc.

Steps:
1. Leaving the skin on, core and grate the apple. Ask an adult to help.
2. Combine apple, oats, milk, apple juice, and lemon juice in a bowl. Cover and put in the refrigerator to sit overnight.
3. Add honey to taste, yogurt, and cinnamon. Mix well.
4. Spoon into bowls and add toppings. Serves 4-6.

The Swiss love celebrations! Christmas begins with chocolate-filled Advent calendars on December 1. It ends with Epiphany, or Three Kings Day, on January 6. Groups sing and carry stars from house to house to represent the guiding star the three kings followed to get to Jesus.

National Day on August 1 is marked with sausage cookouts and fireworks. In mid-September, Alpine villages hold *Dorffests*. These village festivals celebrate the coming of the cows from the mountains. Bulls wear flower wreaths and bells. People yodel, dance, and enjoy a festival that celebrates the best of Switzerland!

DECORATIVE FOOD

Bern's Onion Market takes place each November. Farmers sell onion and garlic braids in the town square. Thousands come to eat onion tarts and buy ropes of onions braided together and shaped into wreaths.

NATIONAL
DAY

1914-1918
Switzerland organizes Red Cross units during World War I

1815
The Swiss Confederation is recognized as a neutral state, avoiding conflict outside its borders

1920
Geneva becomes the headquarters for the League of Nations

1291
Switzerland gains independence when three regions form a partnership to prevent outside control

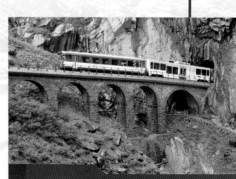

1882
The first rail tunnel through the Alps is finished at St. Gotthard Pass

1971
Women receive the right to vote in Switzerland

2018
Switzerland's largest-ever Olympic team wins 5 gold, 6 silver, and 4 bronze medals at the Winter Olympics in Pyeongchang, South Korea

2012
The scientists at CERN discover more about the Higgs boson, leading to further understanding of space

1990
The world's first web site and Internet server goes live at CERN, the nuclear research facility in Geneva

SWITZERLAND FACTS

Official Name: Swiss Confederation

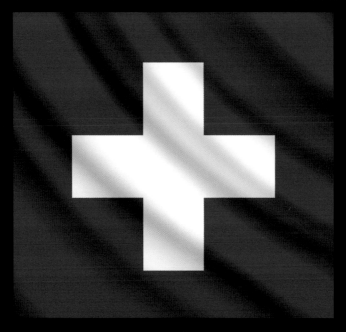

Flag of Switzerland: A square red flag with a white cross in the middle. The arms of the cross are of equal lengths.

Area: 15,937 square miles
  (41,277 square kilometers)

Capital City: Bern

Important Cities: Basel, Geneva, Zurich

Population:
8,236,303 (July 2017)

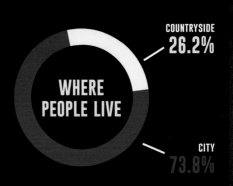

WHERE PEOPLE LIVE

COUNTRYSIDE
26.2%

CITY
73.8%

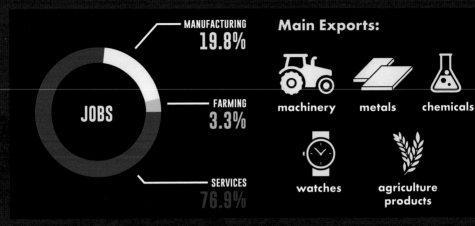

MANUFACTURING
19.8%

JOBS

FARMING
3.3%

SERVICES
76.9%

Main Exports:

machinery

metals

chemicals

watches

agriculture
products

National Holiday:
Swiss National Day (August 1)

Main Languages:
German, French, Italian, Romansch

Form of Government:
federal republic

Title for Country Leader:
president

RELIGION

NONE
23.9%

OTHER
3%

MUSLIM
5.1%

CHRISTIAN
68%

Unit of Money:
Swiss franc

GLOSSARY

alpenhorn—a long, wooden horn once used by herdsmen in the mountains of Switzerland

amateur—related to a person who does something for pleasure and not as a job

burrow—to make a hole or tunnel in the ground by digging

elevation—the height above sea level

ethnicities—groups of people who share customs and an identity

glacier—a massive sheet of ice that covers a large area of land

heritage—the traditions, achievements, and beliefs that are part of the history of a group of people

landlocked—completely surrounded by land

plateau—an area of flat, raised land

refugees—people who flee their homes for safety

resorts—vacation spots that offer recreation, entertainment, and relaxation

rural—related to the countryside

service jobs—jobs that perform tasks for people or businesses

temperate—associated with a mild climate that does not have extreme heat or cold

tortes—rich cakes

tourists—people who travel to visit another place

traditional—related to customs, ideas, or beliefs handed down from one generation to the next

urban—related to cities and city life

yodel—to sing without words while going back and forth between one's natural voice range and a higher range

TO LEARN MORE

AT THE LIBRARY

Levy, Patricia, Richard Lord, and Debbie Nevins. *Switzerland.* New York, N.Y.: Cavendish Square Pub., 2016.

Murray, Julie. *Switzerland.* Minneapolis, Minn.: Big Buddy Books, 2016.

Rogers Seavey, Lura. *Switzerland.* New York, N.Y.: Children's Press, 2017.

ON THE WEB

FACTSURFER

Factsurfer.com gives you a safe, fun way to find more information.

1. Go to www.factsurfer.com.

2. Enter "Switzerland" into the search box.

3. Click the "Surf" button and select your book cover to see a list of related web sites.

INDEX